Spring

LABURNUM
PRESS

Stephen White-Thomson

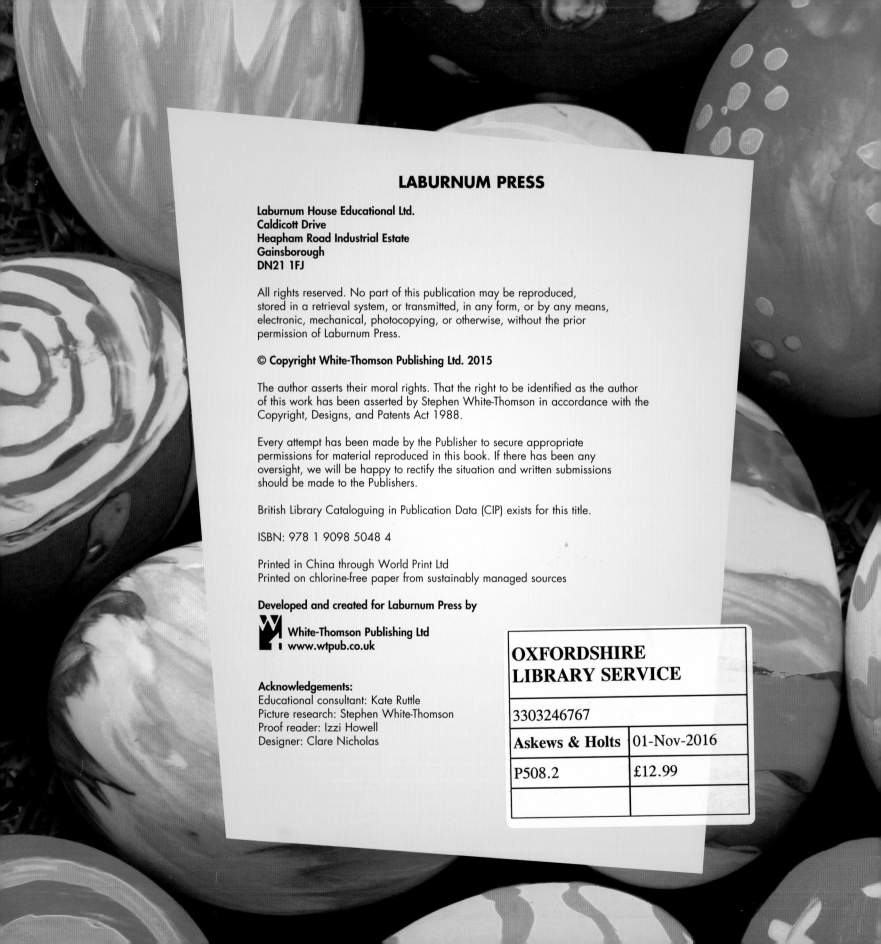

LABURNUM PRESS

Laburnum House Educational Ltd.
Caldicott Drive
Heapham Road Industrial Estate
Gainsborough
DN21 1FJ

British Library Cataloguing in Publication Data (CIP) exists for this title.

ISBN: 978 1 9098 5048 4

Printed in China through World Print Ltd
Printed on chlorine-free paper from sustainably managed sources

Developed and created for Laburnum Press by

White-Thomson Publishing Ltd
www.wtpub.co.uk

Acknowledgements:
Educational consultant: Kate Ruttle
Picture research: Stephen White-Thomson
Proof reader: Izzi Howell
Designer: Clare Nicholas

Contents

Getting Warmer

In spring the weather changes.

Slowly it becomes warmer.

Spring flowers

stem

Why are these flowers called snowdrops?

Why is this called

a carpet of bluebells?

Trees in blossom

Trees come to life again

after the cold winter.

bud

blossom

Which fruit will grow when

the blossom finishes?

Frogs and butterflies

frogspawn

tadpoles

Frogs lay their eggs in ponds in spring.

10

Red Admiral

Which creature

turned into this butterfly?

Spring festivals

Which animal is in the Hindu festival of Holi?

At the Jewish festival of Purim, people dress in beautiful costumes.

Easter

We love to eat chocolate at Easter!

bunny

sweets

14

Which colours do you like to paint your Easter eggs?

15

Special food

What does the cross stand for
on these hot cross buns?

Sometimes we eat simnel cakes at Easter.

marzipan

dried fruit

17

Which material can you get from sheep to make into clothes?

18

In spring, cows go out into the fields to eat the fresh grass.

munch!

19

21

Sparklers books are designed to support and extend the learning of young children. Regular winners of Practical Pre-School silver and gold awards, the books' high-interest subjects link to the Early Years curriculum and beyond. Find out more about Early Years foundation stages (EYFS) at www.gov.uk/government/publications/early-years-foundation-stage-framework–2, and reading with children from the National Literacy Trust (www.literacytrust.org.uk).

Themed titles
Spring is one of four **Seasons** titles that encourage children to learn about the fun and informative aspects of their lives in the different seasons. The other titles are **Autumn** (ISBN: 978 1 9098 5050 7), **Winter** (ISBN: 978 1 9098 5051 4), and **Summer** (ISBN: 978 1 9098 5049 1).

The prime areas of learning: (taught in nurseries)
- communication and language
- physical development
- personal, social and emotional development

The specific areas of learning: (taught in reception classes)
- literacy
- mathematics
- understanding the world
- expressive arts and design

Making the most of reading time
When reading with younger children, take time to explore the pictures together. Ask children to find, identify and count or describe different objects. Point out colours and textures. Allow quiet spaces in your reading so that children can ask questions or repeat your words. Try pausing mid-sentence so that children can predict the next word. This sort of participation develops early reading skills.

Follow the words with your finger as you read. The main text is in Infant Sassoon, a clear, friendly font designed for children learning to read and write. The label and sound effects add fun and give the opportunity to distinguish between levels of communication. Where appropriate, labels, sound effects or main text may be presented phonetically. Encourage children to imitate the sounds.

As you read the book, you can also take the opportunity to talk about the book itself with appropriate vocabulary such as "page", "cover", "back", "front", "label" and "page number".

You can also extend children's learning by using the books as a springboard for discussion and further activities. There are a few suggestions on the facing page.

Pages 4–5

Make a simple weather chart and record how the weather changes. Introduce the children to the idea of a thermometer as something that measures how warm or cold it is. Put a mark when it's a cold day. Wait for a warm day and talk about what has changed.

Pages 5–6

Make cress eggheads. Clean out some boiled eggshells (or use empty yoghurt or crème fraiche pots). Draw faces on the eggshells. Inside each one put a wet wad of kitchen towel with some wet cotton wool above it. Make sure there's a gap between the top of the cotton wool and the edge of the egg. Sprinkle cress seeds on the cotton wool and gently press them in. Place the eggheads in egg-cups on a warm and sunny windowsill and wait for your cress to grow. Then harvest it for sandwiches.

Pages 8–9

Show the children time-lapse photography of blossom opening and becoming fruit. Photographer-gardeners like Neil Bromhill (www.rightplants4me.co.uk) offer a range of videos. Watch how blossom grows, dies and fruit grows.

Pages 10–11

It is no longer recommended that you keep frogspawn in the classroom in a tank because spawn has a better chance of developing into frogs in the wild. However, it is easy and environmentally sustainable now to get hold of caterpillars to 'grow' into butterflies. Find companies online, such as www.insectlore.com, that sell kits including caterpillars and nutrients. Encourage the children to watch carefully, drawing the different stages that they see.

Pages 12–13

Give children large, outline pictures of elephants and encourage them to decorate their elephants too. Show them lots of patterns linked to Holi and talk about the bright, fresh colours that are used. Encourage them to explore a range of media including finger paints and pastels.

Pages 14–15

Use onion skins to colour some eggs. For full details of the recipe, look online. But the main idea is: place onion skins and vinegar in a stainless-steel pan with about 300 ml of water. Put a lid on the pan. Bring to the boil and simmer for about 30 minutes. When the liquid is at room temperature, strain through a sieve, return to the pan and add the eggs. Bring back to the boil and simmer for 30 minutes. Put coloured eggs into the fridge before you decorate them.

Pages 16–17

If you can, take the children to a farm and let them enjoy the young animals. Can they name the young as well as the older animals (e.g. calf-cow, lamb-sheep etc)?

Pages 18–19

Bring hot-cross buns to the setting, together with a variety of jams and spreads. Let the children look at the buns and smell them. Encourage discussion about the cross shape. Slice the buns in half and give the children the opportunity to try spreading them with butter and jam for their snack.

Pages 20 – 21

Depending on where you live, take the children out for a 'signs of spring' walk. As well as looking at budding plants, look for baby animals such as ducklings, goslings or cygnets on ponds, streams and rivers. Encourage the children to listen for cuckoos and to watch for swallows or swifts slicing through the sky. Develop the children's vocabulary giving them interesting words to describe actions as well as what the creatures look like.

Index

Picture acknowledgements:
iStock: 11 (MagMos); **Shutterstock**: 4 (Sergey Novikov), 6 (Roman Samokhin),
7 (Artens); **Thinkstock**: cover (ulkas), 5 (Stockbyte), 8-9 (SerrNovik), 10 (fotostic),
12 (Comstock), 13 (iprostocks), 14 (soumenNath), 15 (ddsign_stock), 16 (fotokostic),
17 (Sponner), 18 (sereznly)cover (ulkas), 19 (iStock), 20 (Przemyslaw Rzeszutko),
21 (Fireglo2). Background to 2, 3, 22, 23, 24 Shutterstock/ballounm